Customs Broker Exam Study Guide &
How to Start Your Own Customs Brokerage Business

Written 2010 by Jon K. Sasaki
Published 2010

For permission to reproduce writings from this book,
please email jon@advocate-sasaki.net.

Customs Broker Exam Study Guide &
        How to Start Your Own Customs Brokerage
        Business
Jon K Sasaki

Business & Economics, Exports & Imports

Disclaimer:

This book is designed to provide guidance regarding the subject matter covered. This information is given with the understanding that the author is not engaged in rendering legal, accounting, or other professional advice.

Contents

Part 1
Customs Broker Exam Study Guide

Contents
Part 2

How to Start Your Own Customs Brokerage Business

Part 1 Introduction

Customs Broker Exam Study Guide by Advocate

Each customs broker has his or her own unique story on how they entered the field. Many, as in my case, begin working in a freight forwarding environment. Others start out as support staff for a customs brokerage department or company. Still others find their way working for a company's import and export compliance team. Whatever the reason, passing the exam and getting one's customs broker license is, without a doubt, considered a major landmark in your career.

In order to become a customs broker there are a few requirements. First, and in general, most people are eligible to apply to become a customs broker, as long as you're at least 21 years of age, a US citizen, and not a federal employee. Second, and the aim of this book, is the requirement of passing the customs broker exam—a four hour open-book test consisting of 80 multiple choice questions requiring 75% to pass. As you may already be aware, the exam is administered twice a year, once on the first Wednesday in April and then again on the first Wednesday in October. Applications for the exam are to be submitted to your nearest service port (the location where you would like to sit for the exam) within at least about a month prior to the test. The application and further instructions are found at Customs' website www.cbp.gov. And, ultimately, upon passing the exam, the applicant is to submit their application to become a customs broker to US Customs.

$ Money Saving Tip $
The 19 CFR and HTS publications are quite expensive investments. So, if you can, find a used copy from work or find someone who has just taken the exam. The variance in content from issue to issue isn't really that significant.

It is said that the average passing rate for the exam, which varies somewhat significantly from year-to-year, is as low as 5%. Whatever the rate may be, your experience can be entirely unique based primarily on your preparation, which makes me want share my experience with the customs broker exam.

A few years ago, I began working for a large freight forwarding company as an air import agent. Basically, this position meant that I performed customer service services for importers upon customs release of their freight. Included in my duties was the function of requesting information from importers at the request of our office's customs brokerage department. After about a year of working and learning in this environment, I heard that a friend of mine, who was currently working in the customs brokerage department, was already studying for and planned on taking the next scheduled exam. I was well aware that even at this point in my young career that I understood little of customs brokerage. However, I smelled an opportunity, and thought even if I didn't pass, it would show some initiative. What the heck, I could always take it as many times as needed until I had mastered it.

So, the day I decided to take my first step, I asked the team leader of the customs brokerage department how he began studying for the exam. Hoping he would say that there was this fool-proof study course available that would most likely secure my chances of passing, I was a little disheartened when he said "just read through the reg's". This meant "read through the nearly 700 pages of the small print, government language laced, behemoth known as title 19 of the code of federal regulations (the 19 cfr)". So, I did. I borrowed an old copy of the 19 cfr from the office, skipped my usual time in front of the television after dinner that evening, to lie down on my bed and started reading the thing. Well, at a certain point, I had read about as much as I could that night, and already I knew that this technique was not going to work.

Later that week I sought additional advice from my friend who was currently in the middle of studying for the exam. He let me borrow some reading material from a course he had ordered on the subject, and also recommended that I review previous exams. So, after browsing through both, I realized two things. One was that his study material was too vague in nature, over-generalized the Customs language, and for nearly $180.00?!?

My other realization was that a majority of the exam questions are going to be coming directly from the 19 cfr and many repeated from one exam to the next. So, the ultimate question was how to filter out the unnecessary parts of the 19 cfr and focus primarily on the items that would appear on the exam. This leads us to our next section on how to most effectively study for the exam and how you may use this book to increase your chances of passing the test—the same proven process and methods that I devised to study for and pass the exam on my first attempt.

$ Money Saving Tip $

Some business's may offer to sell you "deluxe" and more expensive versions of the 19 cfr or harmonized tariff schedule. You will be best off ordering the bare-bones loose leaf forms, and putting them in a large binder from an office supply store.

How to Use This Book

This book, by itself, will probably not guarantee your success on the customs broker exam. It is one of several tools that will best prepare you for the big day. Preparation is the key word and preparedness in context of the customs broker exam means studying as efficiently as possible and on a daily basis. Get gazelle intense as if you didn't want to take the test all over again. Listed below is a kind of checklist of things you should do before getting too far into your studies.

First, go to the following link to Customs' website.

http://www.cbp.gov/xp/cgov/trade/trade_programs /broker/broker_exam/notice_of_exam.xml

Here, you will find links to all the material that Customs says it may draw from when making the exam. Print out all of the following except for the title 19 code of federal regulations (19 cfr) and the harmonized tariff schedule (hts). These two items have too many pages to print. Instead, ask to borrow these items from work or a friend, or purchase from one of the two sources listed in the following section marked "necessary links". Notated below each individual source of testing material in parentheses, are the approximate percentages that questions are pulled from each for the exam.

HTS
(make up approx. 29% of the questions on past 10 exams)

19 CFR
(make up approx. 63% of the questions on past 10 exams)

Customs & Trade Automated Interface Requirements (CATAIR)
(minimal testing from this material on past 10 exams)

Instructions for Preparation of CBP Form 7501
(make up approx. 2% of the questions on past 10 exams)

Submission Changes for Supplemental Information Letters and Post Entry Amendments
(minimal testing from this material on past 10 exams)

Remote Location Filing Requirements
(minimal testing from this material on past 10 exams)

Directives (7 in total)
(make up approx. 5% of the questions on past 10 exams)
- 3510-004: monetary guidelines for setting bond amounts **and its amendment**
- 3550-055: instructions for deriving manufacturer/shipper identification code
- 3550-067: entry summary acceptance and rejection policy

•3550-079A: ultimate consignee at time of entry or release

•3560-001A: census interface-processing procedures

•5610-002A: standard guidelines for the input of names and addresses into the automated commercial system (ACS) files

Make yourself fairly familiar with these items (except for the hts and 19 cfr, which require more involved study and I will further explain here in a bit). You may or may not attempt to commit much of these to memory, but at least be familiar with each in case you have to look something up on these printouts during the actual exam.

Next, begin printing the old exams and exam keys, starting with the most recent. Take a minute to get a feeling of what kinds of questions are asked, how they are presented, etc. Once you get a little more familiar with all the material, you will want to take mock tests using these exams to improve your skills and gauge your progress.

Once you have your 19 cfr available to use, go to the section of this book marked "all sections appearing in exam". In this section of the study guide is a table which lists in order by section, all of the sections tested in the last 10 exams. With a highlighter, begin notating directly into your 19 cfr, the sections and paragraphs that most frequently appear in the exam as indicated on this table. Not only will this improve your familiarity with the 19 cfr and these sections, it will make these items more easily stand out when you are searching for answers.

Once you have your hts, you will want to fixate sticky tabs for all chapters (on the side) and for all sections (on top). The best training method for the hts is simply to go through the old exams and try to classify all the different sorts of merchandise listed throughout the previous exams. This process will expose you to a wide variety of products and materials. It will also help to get you used to the kinds of hts-based questions appearing in exams that require you to check chapter notes, section notes, general notes, and consider the general rules of interpretation (GRI) before deciding on the most appropriate classification/answer.

This study guide also includes a section called "most commonly tested". This section points out parts of the 19 cfr that have most often appeared as questions during the last ten exams. You will want to memorize as much as you can of these. The reason for this is that the more you are able to answer exam questions on the fly (without having to refer to your 19 cfr, hts, directives, etc.), then the more time you will have to focus on the more time-consuming parts such as hts classification.

Necessary Links

Customs website:
www.cbp.gov
>> *past exam and key downloads*
>> *download and print out exam ref's such as directives*
>> *forms for exam and customs broker applications*

Boskage Commerce Publications website:
http://www.boskage.com
>> *for various forms of both 19 cfr and hts*
>> *they also have exam study courses, etc. for the exam,*
>>> *but not cheap*

or try

US government bookstore website:
http://bookstore.gpo.gov/index.jsp
also call 1-866-512-1800
>> *for various forms of both 19 cfr and hts*

Most Commonly Tested
19 CFR

Part 24.23(b)
Fees for processing merchandise
Number of times appearing in last 10 exams: 11
Last appeared in exam: October 2009

The gist of it...

This section outlines the calculation of merchandise processing fees for both formal and informal entries.

Excerpt from 19 CFR...

(b) Fees--(1) Formal entry or release--(i) Ad valorem fee--(A) General. Except as provided in paragraph (c) of this section, merchandise that is formally entered or released is subject to the payment to CBP of an ad valorem fee of 0.21 percent. The 0.21 ad valorem fee is due and payable to CBP by the importer of record of the merchandise at the time of presentation of the entry summary and is based on the value of the merchandise as determined under 19 U.S.C. 1401a. In the case of an express consignment carrier facility or centralized hub facility, each shipment covered by an individual air waybill or bill of lading that is formally entered and valued at $2,000 or less is subject to a $1.00 per individual air waybill or bill of lading fee and, if applicable, to the 0.21 percent ad valorem fee in accordance with paragraph (b)(4) of this section.

(B) Maximum and minimum fees. Subject to the provisions of paragraphs (b)(1)(ii) and (d) of this section relating to the surcharge and to aggregation of the ad valorem fee respectively, the ad valorem fee charged under paragraph (b)(1)(i)(A) of this section shall not exceed $485 and shall not be less than $25............

Most Commonly Tested
19 CFR

152.103(b)
Transaction value—additions to price actually paid
Number of times appearing in last 10 exams: 10
Last appeared in exam: October 2009

The gist of it...
This section states that packing costs, selling commissions, assists, royalties, and proceeds to seller are to be added to the transaction value, otherwise known as the customs value.

Excerpt from 19 CFR...

(b) Additions to price actually paid or payable. (1) The transaction value of imported merchandise is the price actually paid or payable for the merchandise when sold for exportation to the United States, plus amounts equal to:

(i) The packing costs incurred by the buyer with respect to the imported merchandise;

(ii) Any selling commission incurred by the buyer with respect to the imported merchandise;

(iii) The value, apportioned as appropriate, of any assist;

(iv) Any royalty or license fee related to the imported merchandise that the buyer is required to pay, directly or indirectly, as a condition of the sale of the imported merchandise for exportation to the United States; and

(v) The proceeds of any subsequent resale, disposal, or use of the imported merchandise that accrue, directly or indirectly, to the seller............

Most Commonly Tested
19 CFR

152.102(a)
Appraisement of merchandise—defining "assists"
Number of times appearing in last 10 exams: 8
Last appeared in exam: October 2009

The gist of it...

This section states that packing costs, selling commissions, assists, royalties, and proceeds to seller are to be added to the transaction value, otherwise known as the customs value.

Excerpt from 19 CFR...

(a) Assist. (1) ``Assist" means any of the following if supplied directly or indirectly, and free of charge or at reduced cost, by the buyer of imported merchandise for use in connection with the production or the sale for export to the United States of the merchandise:

(i) Materials, components, parts, and similar items incorporated in the imported merchandise.

(ii) Tools, dies, molds, and similar items used in the production of the imported merchandise.

(iii) Merchandise consumed in the production of the imported merchandise.

(iv) Engineering, development, artwork, design work, and plans and sketches that are undertaken elsewhere than in the United States and are necessary for the production of the imported merchandise.

(2) No service or work to which paragraph (a)(1)(iv) of this section applies will be treated as an assist if the service or work:

(i) Is performed by an individual domiciled within the United States;

(ii) Is performed by that individual while acting as an employee or agent of the buyer of the imported merchandise; and

(iii) Is incidental to other engineering, development, artwork, design work, or plans or sketches that are undertaken within the United States.

(3) The following apply in determining the value of assists described in paragraph (a)(1)(iv) of this section:

(i) The value of an assist that is available in the public domain is the cost of obtaining copies of the assist.

(ii) If the production of an assist occurred in the United States and one or more foreign countries, the value of the assist is the value added outside the United States.

(iii) If the assist was purchased or leased by the buyer from an unrelated person, the value of the assist is the cost of the purchase or of the lease..............

Most Commonly Tested
19 CFR

152.103(a)
Transaction value—price actually paid or payable
Number of times appearing in last 10 exams: 6
Last appeared in exam: October 2009

The gist of it...
This section explains that the price actually paid or payable is to be used when determining transaction value for all goods and services involved regardless of after-the-fact changes in price, balances owed, resulting inland freight, etc.

Excerpt from 19 CFR...

(a) Price actually paid or payable--(1) General. In determining transaction value, the price actually paid or payable will be considered without regard to its method of derivation. It may be the result of discounts, increases, or negotiations, or may be arrived at by the application of a formula, such as the price in effect on the date of export in the London Commodity Market. The word ``payable" refers to a situation in which the price has been agreed upon, but actual payment has not been made at the time of importation. Payment may be made by letters of credit or negotiable instruments and may be made directly or indirectly.

Example 1. In a transaction with foreign Company X, a U.S. firm pays Company X $10,000 for a shipment of meat products, packed ready for shipment to the United States. No selling commission, assist, royalty, or license fee is involved. Company X is not related to the U.S. purchaser and imposes no condition or limitation on the buyer.
The customs value of the imported meat products is $10,000--the transaction value of the imported merchandise.
Example 2. A foreign shipper sold merchandise at $100 per unit to a

U.S. importer. Subsequently, the foreign shipper increased its price to $110 per unit. The merchandise was exported after the effective date of the price increase. The invoice price of $100 was the price originally agreed upon and the price the U.S. importer actually paid for the merchandise.

How should the merchandise be appraised?

Actual transaction value of $100 per unit based on the price actually paid or payable.

Example 3. A foreign shipper sells to U.S. wholesalers at one price and to U.S. retailers at a higher price. The shipment undergoing appraisement is a shipment to a U.S. retailer. There are continuing shipments of identical and similar merchandise to U.S. wholesalers.

How should the merchandise be appraised?

Actual transaction value based on the price actually paid or payable by the retailer.

Example 4. Company X in the United States pay $2,000 to Y Toy Factory abroad for a shipment of toys. The $2,000 consists of $1,850 for the toys and $150 for ocean freight and insurance. Y Toy Factory would have charged Company X $2,200 for the toys; however, because Y owed Company X $350, Y charged only $1,850 for the toys. What is the transaction value?

The transaction value of the imported merchandise is $2,200, that is, the sum of the $1,850 plus the $350 indirect payment. Because the transaction value excludes C.I.F. charges, the $150 ocean freight and insurance charge is excluded.

Example 5. A seller offers merchandise at $100, less a 2% discount for cash. A buyer remits $98 cash, taking advantage of the cash discount.

The transaction value is $98, the price actually paid or payable.

(2) Indirect payment. An indirect payment would include the settlement by the buyer, in whole or in part, of a debt owed by the seller, or where the buyer receives a price reduction on a current importation as a means of settling a debt owed him by the seller. Activities such as advertising, undertaken by the buyer on his own account, other than those for which an adjustment is provided in Sec. 152.103(b), will not be considered an indirect payment to the seller though they may benefit the seller. The costs of those activities will not be added to the price actually paid or payable in determining the customs value of the imported merchandise.

(3) Assembled merchandise. The price actually paid or payable may represent an amount for the assembly of imported merchandise in which the seller has no interest other than as the assembler. The price actually paid or payable in that case will be calculated by the addition

21

of the value of the components and required adjustments to form the basis for the transaction value.

Example 1. The importer previously has supplied an unrelated foreign assembler with fabricated components ready for assembly having a value or cost at the assembler's plant of $1.00 per unit. The importer pays the assembler 50[cent] per unit for the assembly. The transaction value for the assembled unit is $1.50.

Example 2. Same facts as Example 1 above except the U.S. importer furnishes to the foreign assembler a tooling assist consisting of a tool acquired by the importer at $1,000. The transportation expenses to the foreign assembler's plant for the tooling assist equal $100. The transaction value for the assembled unit would be $1.50 per unit plus a pro rata share of the tooling assist valued at $1,100.

(4) Rebate. Any rebate of, or other decrease in, the price actually paid or payable made or otherwise effected between the buyer and seller after the date of importation of the merchandise will be disregarded in determining the transaction value under Sec. 152.103(b).

(5) Foreign inland freight and other inland charges incident to the international shipment of merchandise--(i) Ex-factory sales. If the price actually paid or payable by the buyer to the seller for the imported merchandise does not include a charge for foreign inland freight and other charges for services incident to the international shipment of merchandise (an ex-factory price), those charges will not be added to the price.

(ii) Sales other than ex-factory. As a general rule, in those situations where the price actually paid or payable for imported merchandise includes a charge for foreign inland freight, whether or not itemized separately on the invoices or other commercial documents, that charge will be part of the transaction value to the extent included in the price. However, charges for foreign inland freight and other services incident to the shipment of the merchandise to the United States may be considered incident to the international shipment of that merchandise within the meaning of.............

Most Commonly Tested
19 CFR

152.102(f)
Classification and appraisement of merchandise definitions

Number of times appearing in last 10 exams: 5
Last appeared in exam: October 2009

The gist of it...
This section defines the price actually paid or payable as the price actually paid by the buyer to the seller regardless of costs incurred by the shipment process.

Excerpt from 19 CFR...

(f) Price actually paid or payable. ``Price actually paid or payable" means the total payment (whether direct or indirect, and exclusive of any charges, costs, or expenses incurred for transportation, insurance, and related services incident to the international shipment of the merchandise from the country of exportation to the place of importation in the United States) made, or to be made, for imported merchandise by the buyer to, or for the benefit of, the seller........

Most Commonly Tested
19 CFR

132.5(c)
Disposal of merchandise imported in excess of quotas
Number of times appearing in last 10 exams: 5
Last appeared in exam: April 2009

The gist of it...

This section lists the options an importer has to deal with merchandise imported in excess of absolute and tariff-rate quotas.

Excerpt from 19 CFR...

(c) Disposition of excess merchandise. Merchandise imported in excess of either an absolute or a tariff-rate quota may be held for the opening of the next quota period by placing it in a foreign-trade zone or by entering it for warehouse, or it may be exported or destroyed under Customs supervision..........

Most Commonly Tested
19 CFR

111.23(a)
Customs brokers retention of records
Number of times appearing in last 10 exams: 5
Last appeared in exam: April 2009

The gist of it...
This section describes the requirements and required times for keeping records of customs business transactions.

Excerpt from 19 CFR...

(a) Place and period of retention--(1) Place. Records must be retained by a broker in accordance with the provisions of this part and part 163 of this chapter within the broker district that covers the Customs port to which they relate unless the broker chooses to consolidate records at one or more other locations, and provides advance notice of that consolidation to Customs, in accordance with paragraph (b) of this section.

(2) Period. The records described in paragraph (a)(1) of this section, other than powers of attorney, must be retained for at least 5 years after the date of entry. Powers of attorney must be retained until revoked, and revoked powers of attorney and letters of revocation must be retained for 5 years after the date of revocation or for 5 years after the date the client ceases to be an ``active client" as defined in Sec. 111.29(b)(2)(ii), whichever period is later. When merchandise is withdrawn from a bonded warehouse, records relating to the withdrawal
must be retained for 5 years from the date of withdrawal of the last merchandise withdrawn under the entry.........

Most Commonly Tested
19 CFR

152.1(c)
Classification and appraisement of merchandise definitions
Number of times appearing in last 10 exams: 4
Last appeared in exam: April 2009

The gist of it...
This section defines the term "date of exportation" as the date the merchandise leaves the actual country of export and country of origin.

Excerpt from 19 CFR...

(c) Date of exportation. ``Date of exportation," or the ``time of exportation" referred to in section 402, Tariff Act of 1930, as amended (19 U.S.C. 1401a), means the actual date the merchandise finally leaves the country of exportation for the United States. If no positive evidence is at hand as to the actual date of exportation, the port director shall ascertain or estimate the date of exportation by all reasonable ways and means in his power, and in so doing may consider dates on bills of lading, invoices, and other information available to him..........

Most Commonly Tested
19 CFR

142.3a(b)
Format of entry number on entry documentation
Number of times appearing in last 10 exams: 4
Last appeared in exam: October 2009

The gist of it...
This section describes the production of and composition of the entry number for customs entries.

Excerpt from 19 CFR...

(b) Format. The following format, including hyphens, must be used when showing the entry number:

XXX-NNNNNNN-N

XXX represents an entry filer code assigned by CBP, NNNNNNN is a unique
number which is assigned by the broker or importer, and N is a check digit computed from the first 10 characters based on a formula provided by CBP.

(1) Assignment of entry filer code. CBP will assign a unique 3 character (alphabetic, numeric, or alpha numeric) entry filer code to all licensed brokers filing CBP entries. CBP will assign an entry filer code to certain importers filing CBP entries based on importer entry volume, frequency of entry filing, and other considerations. The broker or importer shall use this assigned code as the beginning three characters of the number for all CBP entries, regardless of where the entries are filed.
(2) Entry filer assigned number. For each entry, the broker or importer shall assign a unique 7 digit number. This number shall not be assigned to more than one transaction.
(3) Check digit. The broker or importer is responsible for ensuring that the check digit is computed by data processing equipment..........

Most Commonly Tested
19 CFR

111.30(d)
Duties and responsibilities of customs brokers in regards to the triennial status report
Number of times appearing in last 10 exams: 4
Last appeared in exam: October 2008

The gist of it...

This section outlines when the customs broker status report is due, of what it should consist of, and consequences for not filing in a timely manner.

Excerpt from 19 CFR...

(d) Status report--(1) General. Each broker must file a written status report with Customs on February 1, 1985, and on February 1 of each third year after that date. The report must be accompanied by the fee prescribed in Sec. 111.96(d) and must be addressed to the director of the port through which the license was delivered to the licensee (see Sec. 111.15). A report received during the month of February will be considered filed timely. No form or particular format is required.

(2) Individual. Each individual broker must state in the report required under paragraph (d)(1) of this section whether he is actively engaged in transacting business as a broker. If he is so actively engaged, he must also:

(i) State the name under which, and the address at which, his business is conducted if he is a sole proprietor;

(ii) State the name and address of his employer if he is employed by another broker, unless his employer is a partnership, association or corporation broker for which he is a qualifying member or officer for purposes of Sec. 111.11(b) or (c)(2); and

(iii) State whether or not he still meets the applicable requirements of Sec. 111.11 and Sec. 111.19 and has not engaged in any conduct that could constitute grounds for suspension or revocation under Sec. 111.53.

(3) *Partnership, association or corporation.* Each corporation, partnership or association broker must state in the report required under paragraph (d)(1) of this section the name under which its business as a broker is being transacted, its business address, the name and address of each licensed member of the partnership or licensed officer of the association or corporation who qualifies it for a license under Sec. 111.11(b) or (c)(2), and whether it is actively engaged in transacting business as a broker, and the report must be signed by a licensed member or officer.

(4) *Failure to file timely.* If a broker fails to file the report required under paragraph (d)(1) of this section by March 1 of the reporting year, the broker's license is suspended by operation of law on that date. By March 31 of the reporting year, the port director will transmit written notice of the suspension to the broker by certified mail, return receipt requested, at the address reflected in Customs records. If the broker files the required report and pays the required fee within 60 calendar days of the date of the notice of suspension, the license will be reinstated. If the broker does not file the required report within that 60-day period, the broker's license is revoked by operation of law without prejudice to the filing of an application for a new license. Notice of the revocation will be published in the Customs Bulletin...........

Most Commonly Tested
19 CFR

24.24(a)
Customs accounting and financial procedure—
harbor maintenance fee
Number of times appearing in last 10 exams: 4
Last appeared in exam: October 2007

The gist of it...

This section explains how to calculate the harbor maintenance fee. An extensive list of shipments exempt from the harbor maintenance fee is further described in paragraph (d) of this same section.

Excerpt from 19 CFR...

(a) Fee. Commercial cargo loaded on or unloaded from a commercial vessel is subject to a port use fee of 0.125 percent (.00125) of its value if the loading or unloading occurs at a port within the definition of this section, unless exempt under paragraph (c) of this section or one of the special rules in paragraph (d) of this section is applicable............

Most Commonly Tested
19 CFR

24.1(a)
Customs accounting and financial procedure—collections of duties, taxes, fees, interest, etc.
Number of times appearing in last 10 exams: 4
Last appeared in exam: October 2009

The gist of it...
This section lists the forms of payment accepted by Customs for remittance of duties, etc.

Excerpt from 19 CFR...

(a) Except as provided in paragraph (b) of this section, the following procedure shall be observed in the collection of Customs duties, taxes, fees, interest, and other charges (see Sec. 111.29(b) and 141.1(b) of this chapter):

(1) Any form of United States currency or coin legally current at time of acceptance shall be accepted.

(2) Any bank draft, cashier's check, or certified check drawn on a national or state bank or trust company of the United States or a bank in Puerto Rico or any possession of the United States if such draft or checks are acceptable for deposit by a Federal Reserve bank, branch Federal Reserve bank, or other designated depositary shall be accepted.

(3)(i) An uncertified check drawn by an interested party on a national or state bank or trust company of the United States or a bank in Puerto Rico or any possession of the United States if such checks are acceptable for deposit by a Federal Reserve bank, branch Federal Reserve bank, or other designated depositary shall be accepted if there is on file with the port director a bond to secure the payment of the duties, taxes, fees, interest, or other charges, or if a bond has not been filed, the organization or individual drawing and tendering the uncertified check has been approved by the port director to make payment in such manner. In determining whether an uncertified check shall be accepted in the absence of a bond, the port director shall use available

credit data obtainable without cost to the Government, such as that furnished by banks, local business firms, better business bureaus, or local credit exchanges, sufficient to satisfy him of the credit standing or reliability of the drawer of the check. For purposes of this paragraph, a customs broker who does not have a permit for the district (see the definition of ``district" at Sec. 111.1 of this chapter) where the entry is filed, is an interested party for the purpose of Customs acceptance of such broker's own check, provided the broker has on file the necessary power of attorney which is unconditioned geographically for the performance of ministerial acts. Customs may look to the principal (importer) or to the surety should the check be dishonored.

(ii) If, during the preceding 12-month period, an importer or interested party has paid duties or any other obligation by check and more than one check is returned dishonored by the debtor's financial institution, the port director shall require a certified check, money order or cash from the importer or interested party for each subsequent payment until such time that the port director is satisfied that the debtor has the ability to consistently present uncertified checks that will be honored by the debtor's financial institution.

(4) A U.S. Government check endorsed by the payee to the U.S. Customs Service, a domestic traveler's check, or a U.S. postal, bank, express, or telegraph money order shall be accepted. Before accepting this form of payment the Customs cashier or other employee authorized to receive Customs collections shall require such identification in the way of a current driver's license issued by a state of the United States, or a current passport properly authenticated by the Department of State, or a current credit card issued by one of the numerous travel agencies or clubs, or other credit data, etc., from which he can verify the identity and signature of the person tendering such check or money order.

(5) The face amount of a bank draft, cashier's check, certified check, or uncertified check tendered in accordance with this paragraph shall not exceed the amount due by more than $1 and any required change is authorized to be made out of any available cash funds on hand.

(6) The face amount of a U.S. Government check, traveler's check, or money order tendered in accordance with this paragraph shall not exceed the amount due by more than $50 and any required change is authorized to be made out of any available cash funds on hand.

(7) Credit or charge cards, which have been authorized by the Commissioner of Customs, may be used for the payment of duties, taxes,

fees, and/or other charges at designated Customs-serviced locations. Payment by this manner is limited to non-commercial entries and is subject to ultimate collection from the credit card company. Persons paying by charge or credit card will remain liable for all such charges until paid. Information as to those credit card companies authorized by Customs may be obtained from Customs officers.

(8) Participants in the Automated Broker Interface may use statement processing as described in Sec. 24.25 of this part. Statement processing allows entry/entry summaries and entry summaries to be grouped by either importer or by filer, and allows payment of related duties, taxes and fees by a single payment, rather than by individual checks for each entry. The preferred method of payment for users of statement processing is by Automated Clearinghouse...........

Most Commonly Tested
19 CFR

174.21(b)
Time for review of protests
Number of times appearing in last 10 exams: 3
Last appeared in exam: October 2009

The gist of it...
This section explains the time frame for which Customs has to respond to a protest.

Excerpt from 19 CFR...

(a) In general. Except as provided in paragraph (b) of this section, the port director shall review and act on a protest filed in accordance with section 514, Tariff Act of 1930, as amended (19 U.S.C. 1514), within 2 years from the date the protest was filed. If several timely filed protests are treated as part of a single protest pursuant to Sec. 174.15, the 2-year period shall be deemed to run from the date the last such protest was filed in accordance with section 514, Tariff Act of 1930, as amended (19 U.S.C. 1514).

(b) Protests relating to exclusion of merchandise. If the protest relates to an administrative action involving exclusion of merchandise from entry or delivery under any provision of the Customs laws, the port director shall review and act on a protest filed in accordance with section 514(a)(4), Tariff Act of 1930, as amended (19 U.S.C. 1514(a)(4)), within 30 days from the date the protest was filed. Any protest filed pursuant to this paragraph shall clearly so state on its face. Any protest filed pursuant to this paragraph which is not allowed or denied in whole or in part before the 30th day after the day on which the protest was filed shall be treated as having been denied on such 30th day for purposes of 28 U.S.C. 1581...............

Most Commonly Tested
19 CFR

171.2(b)
Filing petitions for seizures and penalties
Number of times appearing in last 10 exams: 3
Last appeared in exam: October 2009

The gist of it...

This section explains the time frame for which petitions for seizures and penalties must be filed.

Excerpt from 19 CFR...

(b) When filed--(1) Seizures. Petitions for relief from seizures must be filed within 30 days from the date of mailing of the notice of seizure.   (2) Penalties. Petitions for relief from penalties must be filed within 60 days of the mailing of the notice of penalty incurred..............

Most Commonly Tested
19 CFR

152.103(d)
Transaction value and assists
Number of times appearing in last 10 exams: 3
Last appeared in exam: October 2006

The gist of it...

This section outlines what kinds of assists are to be included in the value of the item.

Excerpt from 19 CFR...

(d) Assist. If the value of an assist is to be added to the price actually paid or payable, or to be used as a component of computed value, the port director shall determine the value of the assist and apportion that value to the price of the imported merchandise in the following manner:

(1) If the assist consist of materials, components, parts, or similar items incorporated in the imported merchandise, or items consumed in the production of the imported merchandise, acquired by the buyer from an unrelated seller, the value of the assist is the cost of its acquisition. If the assist were produced by the buyer or a person related to the buyer, its value would be the cost of its production. In either case, the value of the assist would include transportation costs to the place of production.

(2) If the assist consists of tools, dies, molds, or similar items used in the production of the imported merchandise, acquired by the buyer from an unrelated seller,the value of the assist is the cost of its acquisition. If the assist were produced by the buyer or a person related to the buyer, its value would be cost of its production. If the assist has been used previously by the buyer, regardless of whether it had been acquired or produced by him, the original cost of acquisition or production would be adjusted downward to reflect its use before its value could be determined. If the assist were leased by the buyer from an unrelated seller, the value of the assist would be the cost of the lease. In either case, the value of the assist would include

*transportation costs to the place of production. Repairs or
modifications to an assist may increase its value.*

    *Example 1. A U.S. importer supplied detailed designs to the foreign
producer. These designs were necessary to manufacture the merchandise.
The U.S. importer bought the designs from an engineering company in the
U.S. for submission to his foreign supplier.*
    *Should the appraised value of the merchandise include the value of
the assist?*
    *No, design work undertaken in the U.S. may not be added to the price
actually paid or payable.*
    *Example 2. A U.S. importer supplied molds free of charge to the
foreign shipper. The molds were necessary to manufacture merchandise for
the U.S. importer. The U.S. importer had some of the molds manufactured
by a U.S. company and others manufactured in a third country.*
    *Should the appraised value of the merchandise include the value of
the molds?*
    Yes. It is an addition required to be made to transaction value...............

Most Commonly Tested
19 CFR

143.21(a)
Merchandise eligible for informal entry
Number of times appearing in last 10 exams: 3
Last appeared in exam: October 2008

The gist of it...
This section lists the kinds of merchandise for which informal entries can be filed.

Excerpt from 19 CFR...

(a) Shipments of merchandise not exceeding $2,000 in value (except for articles valued in excess of $250 classified in Sections VII, VIII, XI, and XII; Chapter 94 and Chapter 99, Subchapters III and IV, HTSUS);

(b) Any installment, not exceeding $2,000 in value, of a shipment arriving at different times, as described in Sec. 141.82 of this chapter;

(c) A portion of one consignment, when such portion does not exceed $2,000 in value and may be entered separately pursuant to Sec. 141.51 of this chapter. This paragraph does not apply to shipments of articles valued in excess of $250 classified under subheadings from Sections VII, VIII, XI, and XII; or in Chapter 94 and Chapter 99, Subchapters III and IV, HTSUS;

(d) Household or personal effects or tools of trade entitled to free entry under Chapter 98, Subchapter IV, HTSUS (19 U.S.C. 1202);

(e) Household effects used abroad and personal effects whether or not entitled to free entry, not imported in pursuance of a purchase or agreement for purchase and not intended for sale;

(f) Household and personal effects described in paragraph (e) of this section when entered under subheading 9802.00.40, HTSUS (19 U.S.C. 1202), and the value of the repairs and alterations thereto does not exceed $2,000;

(g) Personal effects not exceeding $2,000 in value of citizens of the United States who have died abroad;

(h) Books and other articles classifiable under subheadings 4903.00.00, 4904.00.00, 4905.91.00, 4905.99.00, 9701.10.00, 9701.90.00, 9810.00.05, HTSUS (19 U.S.C. 1202), imported by a library or other institution described in subheadings 9810.00.05 and 9810.00.30, HTSUS (19 U.S.C. 1202);

(i) Theatrical scenery, properties, and effects, motion-picture films, commercial travelers' samples and professional books, implements, instruments, and tools of trade, occupation, or employment, as set forth in Sec. 10.68 of this chapter;

(j) Merchandise which, upon written application to the Commissioner of Customs, is determined to be unique in character or design such that the value thereof cannot be declared and which is not intended for sale or imported in pursuance of a purchase or agreement for purchase; and

(k) Products of the United States, when the aggregate value of the shipment does not exceed $10,000 and the products are imported--

(1) For the purposes of repair or alteration prior to reexportation, or

(2) After having been either rejected or returned by the foreign purchaser to the United States for credit.

(l) Shipments of merchandise qualifying for the administrative exemptions under 19 U.S.C. 1321(a)(2) and provided for in--

(1) Section 10.151 or 145.31 of this chapter (certain importations not exceeding $200 in value);

(2) Section 10.152 or 145.32 of this chapter (certain bona-fide gifts not exceeding $100 in value ($200 in the case of articles sent from a person in the Virgin Islands, Guam, or American Samoa)); or

(3) Section 148.51 or 148.64 of this chapter (certain personal or household articles not exceeding $200 in value)..............

Most Commonly Tested
19 CFR

141.113(b)
Recall of released merchandise—textiles
Number of times appearing in last 10 exams: 3
Last appeared in exam: April 2009

The gist of it...

This section states that time period for which Customs can recall already released textile merchandise.

Excerpt from 19 CFR...

(b) Textiles and textile products. For purposes of determining whether the country of origin of textiles and textile products subject to the provisions of Sec. 102.21 or Sec. 102.22 of this chapter, as applicable, has been accurately represented to CBP, the release from CBP custody of any such textile or textile product shall be deemed conditional during the 180-day period following the date of release. If the port director finds during the conditional release period that a textile or textile product is not entitled to admission into the commerce of the United States because the country of origin of the textile or textile product was not accurately represented to CBP, he shall promptly demand its return to CBP custody. Notwithstanding the provisions of paragraph (h) of this section and Sec. 113.62(m)(1) of this chapter, a failure to comply with a demand for return to CBP custody made under this paragraph shall result in the assessment of liquidated damages equal to the value of the merchandise involved...............

Most Commonly Tested
19 CFR

141.113(a)
Recall of released merchandise—merchandise not legally marked
Number of times appearing in last 10 exams: 3
Last appeared in exam: April 2007

The gist of it...
This section states that time period for which Customs can recall merchandise not properly marked.

Excerpt from 19 CFR...

(a)(1) Merchandise not legally marked. Certain merchandise is required to be marked or labeled pursuant to the following provisions:
(i) Section 304, Tariff Act of 1930, as amended (19 U.S.C. 1304), pertaining to marking with country of origin;
(ii) Textile Fiber Products Identification Act (15 U.S.C. 70);
(iii) Wool Products Labeling Act (15 U.S.C. 68);
(iv) Fur Products Labeling Act (15 U.S.C. 69); and
(v) Chapter 91, Additional U.S. Note 4, Harmonized Tariff Schedule of the United States (HTSUS), pertaining to special marking for watch and clock movements, cases, and dials.
(2) If such merchandise is found after release to be not legally marked, the port director may demand its return to CBP custody for the purpose of requiring it to be properly marked or labeled. The demand for marking or labeling shall be made not later than 30 days after the date of entry in the case of merchandise examined in public stores, and places of arrival, such as docks, wharfs, or piers. Demand may be made no later than 30 days after the date of examination in the case of merchandise examined at the importer's premises or such other appropriate places as determined by the port director...............

Most Commonly Tested
19 CFR

134.1(b)
Country of origin marking definitions
Number of times appearing in last 10 exams: 3
Last appeared in exam: April 2009

The gist of it...

This section states that the "country of origin" of an item will be the country in which it is made, unless further processing of this item in a subsequent country made a significant contribution to changing the basic nature of the item.

Excerpt from 19 CFR...

(b) Country of origin. ``Country of origin'' means the country of manufacture, production, or growth of any article of foreign origin entering the United States. Further work or material added to an article in another country must effect a substantial transformation in order to render such other country the ``country of origin'' within the meaning of this part; however, for a good of a NAFTA country, the NAFTA Marking Rules will determine the country of origin.........

Most Commonly Tested
19 CFR

132.1(a)&(b)
Quotas—definitions
Number of times appearing in last 10 exams: 3
Last appeared in exam: October 2008

The gist of it...
This section defines absolute and tariff rate type quotas.

Excerpt from 19 CFR...

(a) Absolute (or quantitative) quotas. `` *Absolute (or quantitative) quotas" are those which permit a limited number of units of specified merchandise to be entered or withdrawn for consumption during specified periods. Once the quantity permitted under the quota is filled, no further entries or withdrawals for consumption of merchandise subject to quota are permitted. Some absolute quotas limit the entry or withdrawal of merchandise from particular countries (geographic quotas) while others are global quotas and limit the entry or withdrawal of merchandise not by source but by total quantity.*

(b) Tariff-rate quotas. `` *Tariff-rate quotas" permit a specified quantity of merchandise to be entered or withdrawn for consumption at a reduced duty rate during a specified period...............*

Most Commonly Tested
19 CFR

113.27(a)
Effective date of termination of bond by principle
Number of times appearing in last 10 exams: 3
Last appeared in exam: April 2007

The gist of it...
This section specifies when a principal's bond will officially be terminated.

Excerpt from 19 CFR...

(a) Termination by principal. A request by a principal to terminate a bond shall be made in writing to the port director or drawback office in the case of a bond relating to repayment of erroneous drawback payment where the bond was approved. The termination shall take effect on the date requested if the date is at least 10 business days after the date of receipt of the request. Otherwise the termination shall be effective on the close of business 10 business days after the request is received at the port or drawback office. If no termination date is requested, the termination shall take effect on the tenth business day following the date of receipt of the request by the port director, or drawback office in the case of bonds relating to repayment of erroneous drawback payment..............

Most Commonly Tested
19 CFR

111.19(c)
Fees due by customs broker for permit
Number of times appearing in last 10 exams: 3
Last appeared in exam: October 2009

The gist of it...

This section outlines fees due for district and national permits.

Excerpt from 19 CFR...

(c) Fees. Each application for a district permit under paragraph (b) of this section must be accompanied by the $100 and $138 fees specified in Sec. Sec. 111.96(b) and (c). In the case of an application for a national permit under paragraph (f) of this section, the $100 fee specified in Sec. 111.96(b) and the $138 fee specified in Sec. 111.96(c) must be paid at the port through which the applicant's license was delivered (see Sec. 111.15) prior to submission of the application. The $138 fee specified in Sec. 111.96(c) also must be paid in connection with the issuance of an initial district permit concurrently with the issuance of a license under paragraph (a) of this section..............

Most Commonly Tested
19 CFR

111.19(b)
Submission of application for district permit
Number of times appearing in last 10 exams: 3
Last appeared in exam: October 2009

The gist of it...

This section lists required information for district permit application.

Excerpt from 19 CFR...

(b) Submission of application for initial or additional district permit. A broker who intends to conduct customs business at a port within another district for which he does not have a permit, or a broker who was not concurrently granted a permit with the broker's license under paragraph (a) of this section, and except as otherwise provided in paragraph (f) of this section, must submit an application for a permit in a letter to the director of the port at which he intends to conduct customs business. Each application for a permit must set forth or attach the following:

(1) The applicant's broker license number and date of issuance;

(2) The address where the applicant's office will be located within the district and the telephone number of that office;

(3) A copy of a document which reserves the applicant's business name with the state or local government;

(4) The name of the individual broker who will exercise responsible supervision and control over the customs business transacted in the district;

(5) A list of all other districts for which the applicant has a permit to transact customs business;

(6) The place where the applicant's brokerage records will be retained and the name of the applicant's designated recordkeeping contact (see Sec. Sec. 111.21 and 111.23); and

(7) A list of all persons who the applicant knows will be employed in the district, together with the specific employee information prescribed..............

Most Commonly Tested
19 CFR

111.28(c)
Responsible supervision of customs broker—termination of qualifying member or officer
Number of times appearing in last 10 exams: 3
Last appeared in exam: October 2008

The gist of it...
This section describes the responsibility of the customs broker when their employment terminates as an officer of a partnership or corporation.

Excerpt from 19 CFR...

(c) Termination of qualifying member or officer. In the case of an individual broker who is a qualifying member of a partnership for purposes of Sec. 111.11(b) or who is a qualifying officer of an association or corporation for purposes of Sec. 111.11(c)(2), that individual broker must immediately provide written notice to the Assistant Commissioner when his employment as a qualifying member or officer terminates and must send a copy of the written notice to the director of each port through which a permit has been granted to the partnership, association, or corporation..............

Most Commonly Tested
19 CFR

111.29(a)
Due diligence by customs broker in payment
Number of times appearing in last 10 exams: 3
Last appeared in exam: April 2008

The gist of it...

This section states the responsibilities of the customs broker in making payments to customs on behalf of their customers.

Excerpt from 19 CFR...

(a) Due diligence by broker. Each broker must exercise due diligence in making financial settlements, in answering correspondence, and in preparing or assisting in the preparation and filing of records relating to any customs business matter handled by him as a broker. Payment of duty, tax, or other debt or obligation owing to the Government for which the broker is responsible, or for which the broker has received payment from a client, must be made to the Government on or before the date that payment is due. Payments received by a broker from a client after the due date must be transmitted to the Government within 5 working days from receipt by the broker. Each broker must provide a written statement to a client accounting for funds received for the client from the Government, or received from a client where no payment to the Government has been made, or received from a client in excess of the Governmental or other charges properly payable as part of the client's customs business, within 60 calendar days of receipt. No written statement is required if there is actual payment of the funds by a broker..............

Most Commonly Tested
19 CFR

111.45(a)
Revocation by operation of law—license
Number of times appearing in last 10 exams: 3
Last appeared in exam: April 2009

The gist of it...

This section describes the time limit for which a partnership, association, or corporation can operate without a licensed customs broker.

Excerpt from 19 CFR...

(a) License. If a broker that is a partnership, association, or corporation fails to have, during any continuous period of 120 days, at least one member of the partnership or at least one officer of the association or corporation who holds a valid individual broker's license, that failure will, in addition to any other sanction that may be imposed under this part, result in the revocation by operation of law of the license and any permits issued to the partnership, association, or corporation. The Assistant Commissioner or his designee will notify the broker in writing of an impending revocation by operation of law under this section 30 calendar days before the revocation is due to occur................

Most Commonly Tested
19 CFR

111.12(a)
Submission of application for customs broker license
Number of times appearing in last 10 exams: 3
Last appeared in exam: October 2008

The gist of it...
This section outlines the process for applying for ones customs broker license.

Excerpt from 19 CFR...

(a) Submission of application and fee. An application for a broker's license must be submitted in duplicate to the director of the port where the applicant intends to do business. The application must be under oath and executed on Customs Form 3124. The application must be accompanied by the $200 application fee prescribed in Sec. 111.96(a) and one copy of the appropriate attachment required by the application form (Articles of Agreement or an affidavit signed by all partners, Articles of Agreement of the association, or the Articles of Incorporation). If the applicant proposes to operate under a trade or fictitious name in one or more States, evidence of the applicant's authority to use the name in each of those States must accompany the application. An application for an individual license must be submitted within the 3-year period after the applicant took and passed the written examination referred to in Sec. Sec. 111.11(a)(4) and 111.13. The port director may require an individual applicant to provide a copy of the notification that he passed the written examination (see Sec. 111.13(e)) and will require the applicant to submit fingerprints on form FD 258 or electronically at the time of filing the application. The port director may reject an application as improperly filed if the application, on its face, demonstrates that one or more of the basic requirements set forth in Sec. 111.11 have not been met at the time of filing, in which case the application and fee will be returned to the filer without further action.................

Most Commonly Tested
19 CFR

111.11(a)
Customs Brokers—basic requirements for a license
Number of times appearing in last 10 exams: 3
Last appeared in exam: April 2007

The gist of it...
This section lists the requirements for becoming a licensed customs broker.

Excerpt from 19 CFR...

(a) Individual. In order to obtain a broker's license, an individual must:

(1) Be a citizen of the United States on the date of submission of the application referred to in Sec. 111.12(a) and not an officer or employee of the United States Government;

(2) Attain the age of 21 prior to the date of submission of the application referred to in Sec. 111.12(a);

(3) Be of good moral character; and

(4) Have established, by attaining a passing (75 percent or higher) grade on a written examination taken within the 3-year period before submission of the application referred to in Sec. 111.12(a), that he has sufficient knowledge of customs and related laws, regulations and procedures, bookkeeping, accounting, and all other appropriate matters to render valuable service to importers and exporters.................

Most Commonly Tested
19 CFR

102.21(b)
Rules of origin—textiles definitions
Number of times appearing in last 10 exams: 3
Last appeared in exam: April 2009

The gist of it...

In this section Customs gives their definitions of country of origin as it pertains to textiles.

Excerpt from 19 CFR...

(b) Definitions. The following terms will have the meanings indicated when used in this section:

(1) Country of origin. The term country of origin means the country, territory, or insular possession in which a good originates or of which a good is the growth, product, or manufacture.

(2) Fabric-making process. A fabric-making process is any manufacturing operation that begins with polymers, fibers, filaments (including strips), yarns, twine, cordage, rope, or fabric strips and results in a textile fabric.

(3) Knit to shape. The term knit to shape applies to any good of which 50 percent or more of the exterior surface area is formed by major parts that have been knitted or crocheted directly to the shape used in the good, with no consideration being given to patch pockets, appliques, or the like. Minor cutting, trimming, or sewing of those major parts will not affect the determination of whether a good is ``knit to shape."

(4) Major parts. The term major parts means integral components of a good but does not include collars, cuffs, waistbands, plackets, pockets, linings, paddings, trim, accessories, or similar parts.

(5) Textile or apparel product. A textile or apparel product is any good classifiable in Chapters 50 through 63, Harmonized Tariff Schedule of the United States (HTSUS), and any good classifiable under one of the following HTSUS headings or subheadings:

3005.90
3921.12.15
3921.13.15
3921.90.2550
4202.12.40-80
4202.22.40-80
4202.32.40-95
4202.92.05
4202.92.15-30
4202.92.60-90
6405.20.60
6406.10.77
6406.10.90
6406.99.15
6501
6502
6504
6505.90
6601.10-99
7019.19.15
7019.19.28
7019.40-59
8708.21
8804
9113.90.40
9404.90
9612.10.9010

(6) *Wholly assembled.* The term ``wholly assembled'' when used with reference to a good means that all components, of which there must be at least two, preexisted in essentially the same condition as found in the finished good and were combined to form the finished good in a single country, territory, or insular possession. Minor attachments and minor embellishments (for example, appliques, beads, spangles, embroidery, buttons) not appreciably affecting the identity of the good, and minor subassemblies (for example, collars, cuffs, plackets, pockets), will not affect the status of a good as ``wholly assembled'' in a single country, territory, or insular possession.................

Most Commonly Tested
19 CFR

24.23(c)
Customs financial and accounting procedure—receipts
Number of times appearing in last 10 exams: 3
Last appeared in exam: October 2009

The gist of it...
This section describes Customs' procedure for issuing receipts for payments

Excerpt from 19 CFR...

(c) A copy of a Customs bill validated as paid will not normally be provided a payer. If a bill is paid by check, the copy of the Customs bill identified as ``Payer's Copy'' and the payer's cancelled check shall constitute evidence of such payment to Customs. Should a payer desire evidence of receipt, both the ``U.S. Customs Service Copy'' and the ``Payer's Copy'' of the bill and, in the case of payments by mail, a stamped, self-addressed envelope, shall be submitted. The ``Payer's Copy'' of the bill shall then be marked paid by the appropriate Customs official and returned to the payer.................

All Sections Appearing on Exam
19 CFR

The following table represents parts, sections or paragraphs, subsections, and their numbers as they appear in the last 10 exams. The table is arranged by part, then by section, and then by exam date with the most recent exams appearing first for repeating subsections. As you can see from the table on the following page, we start from part 4, as part 0, "Transferred or Delegated Authority", has not appeared in any of the last 10 exams, and it is safe to say that although you can be aware that this part exists, there is no need to memorize anything in it. If a part's subsection or number is blank on the table, then the answer may involve more than one subsection.

The best way to make use of this table is as follows. First, feel free to remove the 19 cfr parts that do not appear below from your 19 cfr binder. You can move these extra parts to a different folder that you can label "just in case". That way, when test time comes, you can reduce the amount of paper you must flip through to get to the sections if necessary to lookup.

Next, go through the remaining part of your newly condensed 19 cfr, and with a highlighter, highlight the sections and subsections that appear in this table. This will allow these lines to jump out at you when you're scanning through the pages of your reg's for your answers.

$ Money Saving Tip $
Tell your employer that you're interested in taking the exam. Ask if they could help pay for expenses. Or, they may do so on the condition that you pass in order to get reimbursed.

Exam Date	Part	Section	Subsection	Number
2008 April	4	37	A	
2008 October	4	37	B	
2008 October	4	37		
2005 April	7	3	A	
2009 October	10	8	A	
2009 April	10	13		
2009 April	10	14		
2009 April	10	16		
2008 April	10	31	A	3
2006 April	10	31	F	
2007 October	10	37		
2005 April	10	37		
2008 October	10	39	F	
2007 April	10	39	F	
2005 April	10	46		
2006 April	10	101	D	
2005 October	10	101	D	
2008 April	10	151		
2008 April	10	153		
2008 October	10	171		

Exam Date	Part	Section	Subsection	Number
2007 April	10	178	B	2
2005 October	10	178	B	2
2006 October	10	216	A	
2009 April	10	222		
2007 April	10	223	A	3
2008 October	10	457		
2008 October	11	12	B	
2008 October	12	1		
2008 October	12	3		
2008 October	12	4		
2007 April	12	8	A	
2008 October	12	41	A	
2005 April	12	118		
2005 April	12	118		
2005 April	12	120		
2009 April	12	121	A	
2005 April	12	121		
2008 October	18	5	F	
2006 October	18	6	B	
2006 October	18	8	B	
2008 April	18	10		
2006 October	18	10		
2007 April	18	12	A	
2008 April	18	20		
2008 April	19	1	A	3
2006 October	19	1	A	11
2006 October	19	2	E	
2008 April	19	4	B	4
2007 April	19	11	D	
2005 April	19	11	D	
2008 April	19	12	D	3
2009 April	19			
2006 April	24	1	A	8
2005 October	24	1	A	3
2005 April	24	1	A	8
2009 October	24	1	A	3
2006 April	24	1	C	
2008 October	24	1		
2006 October	24	1		

Exam Date	Part	Section	Subsection	Number
2009 October	24	3	A	
2007 April	24	3	E	
2005 October	24	3	E	
2006 April	24	4	C	
2006 April	24	5	A	
2007 April	24	5	E	
2007 October	24	5		
2005 October	24	5		
2005 April	24	5		
2006 April	24	12	A	2
2009 October	24	23	A	
2008 October	24	23	B	1
2008 October	24	23	B	1
2008 October	24	23	B	1
2007 October	24	23	B	
2007 October	24	23	B	
2006 October	24	23	B	1
2006 April	24	23	B	1
2006 April	24	23	B	
2005 April	24	23	B	
2005 April	24	23	B	2
2009 October	24	23	B	
2008 October	24	23	C	
2008 April	24	23	C	
2009 October	24	23	C	
2008 October	24	23		
2007 October	24	24	A	
2007 October	24	24	A	2
2006 April	24	24	A	
2006 April	24	24	A	
2009 April	24	24	B	1
2006 October	24	24	B	1
2005 October	24	24	E	2
2009 October	24	24	E	2
2008 October	24	24		
2005 April	24	24		
2008 October	24	25	C	
2008 April	24	25	C	3
2009 April	24	25		

Exam Date	Part	Section	Subsection	Number
2005 October	101	3	B	1
2006 October	101	5		
2006 April	102	1	D	
2007 April	102	1	G	5
2007 April	102	1	K	
2009 October	102	1	K	
2009 April	102	11	A	3
2008 October	102	11	A	3
2009 April	102	11	B	1
2008 October	102	11	B	1
2006 October	102	13	A	
2007 October	102	13		
2009 October	102	13		
2009 October	102	13		
2007 October	102	15		
2009 October	102	15		
2009 April	102	20	F	
2008 October	102	20	F	
2005 April	102	20		
2009 April	102	21	B	5
2008 April	102	21	B	5
2008 April	102	21	B	5
2008 April	102	21	C	
2008 April	111	1		
2007 October	111	1		
2007 October	111	1		
2006 October	111	1		
2005 October	111	1		
2008 April	111	2	A	II
2006 October	111	2	A	
2007 April	111	11	A	4
2007 April	111	11	A	4
2005 April	111	11	A	1
2008 October	111	12	A	
2007 April	111	12	A	
2005 April	111	12	A	
2007 April	111	15		
2006 October	111	19	B	
2006 April	111	19	B	

Exam Date	Part	Section	Subsection	Number
2009 October	111	19	B	
2005 October	111	19	C	
2005 October	111	19	C	
2009 October	111	19	C	
2005 April	111	19	D	
2009 October	111	19	F	4
2009 April	111	23	A	
2007 April	111	23	A	
2006 April	111	23	A	2
2005 October	111	23	A	2
2005 April	111	23	A	2
2009 October	111	23	B	2
2008 April	111	24		
2005 April	111	24		
2009 October	111	24		
2009 April	111	25		
2007 April	111	28	B	1
2007 April	111	28	B	1
2006 October	111	28	B	2
2008 October	111	28	C	
2008 April	111	28	C	
2007 October	111	28	C	
2007 October	111	28		
2009 April	111	29	A	
2008 April	111	29	A	
2006 October	111	29	A	
2006 April	111	29		
2005 October	111	30	C	
2008 October	111	30	D	
2007 October	111	30	D	
2006 October	111	30	D	1
2006 April	111	30	D	
2009 October	111	30		
2005 April	111	41	B	
2005 April	111	42	B	
2009 April	111	45	A	
2006 October	111	45	A	
2005 October	111	45	A	
2005 October	111	45	B	

Exam Date	Part	Section	Subsection	Number
2008 October	111	45		
2006 October	111	53		
2009 April	111	91	B	
2006 October	111	91	B	
2007 April	111	239	A	2
2008 October	112	12	A	
2006 October	113	3		
2007 October	113	4		
2006 October	113	11		
2005 April	113	12	B	I
2006 October	113	13	A	
2009 October	113	13		
2005 April	113	24	1	
2005 April	113	24	2	
2005 April	113	24	3	
2009 April	113	24	A	
2006 April	113	24	A	
2005 April	113	24	B	
2005 April	113	24	D	
2007 April	113	26	A	
2006 October	113	27	A	
2006 April	113	27	A	
2007 April	113	27	B	
2006 April	113	27	B	
2007 April	113	55	A	1
2005 April	113	55	A	1
2005 April	113	62	I	
2009 April	113	62		
2005 October	113	62		
2005 October	113	72		
2007 April	113	129	B	
2008 October	114	3	A	
2008 October	114	3	B	
2007 October	114	3		
2009 April	114	22		
2006 October	114	22		
2007 April	114	23	A	
2009 October	114	25		
2007 October	114	31	A	

Exam Date	Part	Section	Subsection	Number
2006 October	114	31	A	
2008 October	122	50	B	
2008 October	122	50		
2008 April	122	119	B	
2007 October	122	119	B	
2008 October	123	10	B	
2008 October	123	10		
2005 April	123	92	A	1
2009 October	123	92	A	1
2005 April	123	92	B	
2009 October	127	1	C	
2006 October	127	12	A	2
2005 April	127	12		
2005 April	127	28	C	
2005 April	128	11	B	7
2008 October	128	24	A	
2008 October	132	1	A	
2006 April	132	1	A	
2006 April	132	1	B	
2008 October	132	1		
2009 April	132	3		
2005 October	132	3		
2006 April	132	4		
2008 October	132	5	B	
2009 April	132	5	C	
2008 October	132	5	C	
2006 October	132	5	C	
2006 April	132	5	C	
2005 October	132	5	C	
2006 April	132	5		
2006 April	132	5		
2006 October	132	11	A	
2008 October	132	11		
2006 April	132	11		
2008 October	132	12		
2008 October	132	12		
2008 October	132	12		
2006 April	132	12		
2006 April	132	12		

Exam Date	Part	Section	Subsection	Number
2008 October	132	14		
2007 October	132	22		
2008 April	133	12	B	
2008 April	133	13	A	
2006 April	133	21		
2006 October	133	23		
2006 October	133	27		
2009 October	133	27		
2009 April	133	34	B	
2007 April	133	52	B	
2009 April	134	1	B	
2008 October	134	1	B	
2008 October	134	1	B	
2008 April	134	2		
2005 April	134	32	D	
2009 October	134	32	D	
2007 April	134	33		
2006 April	134	33		
2005 October	134	33		
2007 October	134	42		
2008 October	134	45		
2008 October	134	46		
2008 April	134	46		
2007 October	134	46		
2008 April	134	52	A	
2008 October	134	54	A	
2009 April	134			
2007 April	141	0	A	I
2007 October	141	1		
2008 October	141	5		
2007 October	141	5		
2007 April	141	5		
2006 April	141	11		
2007 April	141	12		
2007 October	141	31	D	
2005 October	141	34		
2005 April	141	34		
2005 October	141	35		
2007 October	141	36		

Exam Date	Part	Section	Subsection	Number
2007 October	141	36		
2007 October	141	37		
2007 October	141	37		
2005 April	141	43		
2006 October	141	57	D	2
2009 April	141	57		
2006 October	141	61	A	2
2005 October	141	61	D	3
2008 October	141	68	C	
2005 April	141	69	B	
2005 April	141	83		
2005 April	141	86	A	10
2008 April	141	86		
2005 October	141	86		
2009 April	141	89	A	
2005 April	141	89		
2007 April	141	113	A	
2007 April	141	113	A	
2005 October	141	113	A	
2009 April	141	113	B	
2008 April	141	113	B	
2008 April	141	113	B	
2008 April	141	113	H	
2007 October	141	0		
2007 April	142	2	A	
2006 April	142	3	A	
2005 April	142	3	A	I
2009 October	142	3	A	B
2005 April	142	3	B	
2008 April	142	6	A	
2005 October	142	6		
2005 April	142	6		
2009 October	142	11	A	
2005 April	142	12	A	
2005 April	142	12	B	
2005 April	142	14	A	
2007 October	142	15		
2007 April	142	15		
2009 October	142	15		

Exam Date	Part	Section	Subsection	Number
2009 October	142	17		
2009 October	142	21	B	3
2008 October	142	21	E	
2007 October	142	21		
2009 October	142	21		
2007 October	142	22		
2009 October	142	22		
2009 October	142	25	A	
2008 April	142	26	A	
2005 April	142	26	A	
2009 April	142	28	A	
2007 April	143	13		
2007 April	143	16		
2008 October	143	21	A	
2008 October	143	21	A	
2007 October	143	21	A	
2007 October	143	21	K	1
2008 October	143	21		
2008 October	143	21		
2008 April	143	21		
2007 April	143	21		
2006 April	143	21		
2009 October	143	23	J	
2009 April	144	5		
2008 October	144	5		
2007 October	144	5		
2007 April	144	5		
2006 October	144	5		
2006 April	144	5		
2006 October	144	32	A	
2008 April	144	33		
2009 October	144	34	A	
2005 October	144	37	H	3
2006 April	144	41	G	
2009 April	146	25		
2005 October	146	32	A	
2008 October	146	32		
2009 April	146	35	E	
2007 October	146	43	B	

Exam Date	Part	Section	Subsection	Number
2007 October	146	43		
2008 April	146	44	D	
2007 October	146	44		
2008 October	146	52	A	
2007 October	146	65		
2009 April	146	67	C	
2006 April	146			
2007 October	147	0		
2007 October	147	B		
2005 April	148	53	A	
2007 April	151	11		
2009 April	152	1	C	
2007 April	152	1	C	
2005 October	152	1	C	
2005 April	152	1	C	
2007 October	152	1		
2007 April	152	13	A	
2007 April	152	13	C	
2006 October	152	23		
2007 October	152	25		
2005 October	152	101	B	4
2005 April	152	101	C	
2009 April	152	101	D	
2007 October	152	101	D	
2006 October	152	101		
2008 April	152	102	A	1
2008 April	152	102	A	2
2006 October	152	102	A	
2005 October	152	102	A	
2005 October	152	102	A	1
2005 October	152	102	A	1
2005 October	152	102	A	1
2005 April	152	102	A	
2007 April	152	102	F	
2005 October	152	102	F	
2005 April	152	102	F	
2009 October	152	102	F	
2009 October	152	102	F	
2007 October	152	102		

66

Exam Date	Part	Section	Subsection	Number
2009 October	152	102		
2008 October	152	103	A	
2007 April	152	103	A	1
2005 October	152	103	A	
2005 October	152	103	A	1
2005 April	152	103	A	
2009 October	152	103	A	
2008 October	152	103	B	IV
2007 October	152	103	B	1
2007 October	152	103	B	
2007 October	152	103	B	
2007 April	152	103	B	1
2007 April	152	103	B	
2006 October	152	103	B	III
2005 October	152	103	B	
2005 April	152	103	B	I THRU V
2009 October	152	103	B	
2009 October	152	103	C	2
2006 October	152	103	D	2
2005 October	152	103	D	1
2005 October	152	103	D	2
2008 October	152	103	F	
2008 October	152	103	I	
2009 October	152	103	J	
2008 October	152	103	M	
2009 April	152	103		
2007 October	152	103		
2006 October	152	103		
2006 October	152	103		
2005 April	152	103		
2005 April	152	103		
2009 October	152	103		
2005 October	152	105	B	
2009 October	152	106		
2008 October	152	108		
2005 April	158	2		
2009 October	158	2		
2005 April	158	11		
2005 April	158	12	B	

Exam Date	Part	Section	Subsection	Number
2006 April	159	1		
2005 April	159	2		
2006 October	159	3		
2006 October	159	9	C	1
2005 October	159	9	D	
2006 October	159	11	A	
2008 October	159	11		
2006 October	159	12		
2005 April	159	22	C	
2009 October	159	32	D	
2009 April	159	32		
2007 October	159	32		
2007 October	159	32		
2006 April	159	32		
2005 April	159	32		
2005 April	159	33		
2007 April	159	34	A	
2007 April	159	34	A	
2007 April	159	34	B	2
2008 October	159	41		
2008 October	159	47		
2009 April	161	5		
2009 October	162	23	A	1
2008 April	162	73	A	2
2006 April	162	73	A	3
2006 April	162	74	A	2
2008 April	162	74	B	
2006 April	162	74	C	
2005 October	162	74	IV	1
2008 October	162	74		
2007 April	162	74		
2005 October	162	74		
2006 April	162	75	A	
2006 April	162	75	B	
2007 April	163	1		
2008 April	163	4	B	1
2007 April	163	4	B	1
2007 April	163	5	B	2
2005 October	163	5	B	1

Exam Date	Part	Section	Subsection	Number
2009 October	163	6	B	
			SUBPART	
2007 October	163	6	G	
2009 October	163	6		
2008 April	163	9		
2008 April	163	APPENDIX		
2006 April	171	2	A	
2008 April	171	2	B	1
2006 April	171	2	B	1
2009 October	171	2	B	1
2006 April	171	32		
2009 April	171	61		
2006 April	171	APP B	G	
2006 October	171	APP B	K	
2006 April	171	APP C	IV	
2009 October	171	APPENDIX A I 2 C		
		APPENDIX B		
2007 April	171			
2005 October	171	APPENDIX C	SECTION II	D
			SECTION	
2005 October	171	APPENDIX C	XI	C
2007 April	171	APPENDIX C	V	E
2008 April	172	1	A	
2006 October	172	3	B	
2009 April	172	3		
2007 April	172	22	A	
2007 April	172	22	B	
2009 April	172	31		
2009 April	172	41		
2009 April	174	3	C	
2005 October	174	11		
2009 April	174	21	B	
2007 October	174	21	B	
2009 October	174	21	B	
2008 October	174	31		
2007 October	174	31		
2007 April	177	11	B	2
2005 April	181	11	B	
2009 April	181	21	B	

Exam Date	Part	Section	Subsection	Number
2007 October	181	22	A	
2009 April	181	22	C	
2009 October	181	22	C	
2005 April	181	22	D	III
2006 April	181	22		
2008 October	181	31		
2007 October	181	31		
2006 April	181	31		
2006 April	181	31		
2009 April	181	32	B	
2008 October	181	32		
2006 October	181	42		
2009 October	181	44	A	
2006 October	181	44		
2006 October	181	45	B	
2005 October	181	45	B	1
2006 April	181	49		
2005 October	181	53	A	III
2005 October	181	53	A	III
2009 April	181	APPENDIX	PART II	SEC 4
2007 April	191	6		
2006 October	191	14		
2006 April	191	14		
2008 April	191	15		
2007 October	191	15		
2008 April	191	23		
2007 October	191	24		
2007 April	191	28		
2005 October	191	28		
2005 October	191	33	A	
2005 October	191	33		
2005 October	191	34	A	
2005 October	191	34		
2007 April	191	35	A	
2005 October	191	35	A	
2006 April	191	35		
2005 October	191	41		
2007 October	191	51	C	4
2006 October	191	51	E	I

Exam Date	Part	Section	Subsection	Number
2007 October	191	52	C	
2006 April	191	52		
2005 October	191	82		
2007 October	191	84		
2007 April	191	92	D	
2007 October	191	92		
2006 April	191	92		
2007 April	191	181		
2007 April	191	182		
2009 April	351	212	E	
2009 April	351	402	F	III
2009 April	351	402	F	2
2009 April	351	402	F	2

Part 2 Introduction
How to Start Your Own Customs Brokerage Business

Most customs brokers have thought to themselves at least once, "what it would be like to start and run my own customs brokerage business?". Well, once you have a little experience under your belt, develop the determination to go out on your own, and acquire some resources and patience to allow your business to grow (because it will take some patience), then this books will end up saving you much wasted time and frustration.

The reason I wrote this book is that when I first decided to start my own customs brokerage business, instructions on doing so from Customs or the customs brokerage community were nowhere to be found. I made a conscious declaration to log and document all the steps that I took in order to set up my own customs brokerage business from start to finish. I knew that doing so would invaluable for others following the same path and looking for guidance along the way.

$ Money Saving Tip $
You don't need to pay for a new checking account. Many banks offer free checking, with free checks and a debit card for your new small business. ACH services may be extra, so shop around.

So, with this book, you get to bypass the trial and error method that I used when setting up my own customs brokerage business. This book systematically outlines, step-by-step, how to most efficiently open your own customs brokerage business—and how to do it on a budget.

You may have a long list of prospective customers that you can switch over to your new operation. You may have none. Either way, your ambition to offer a service, superior to any other in your market will, by itself, grow your business. Just use this book for direction, stick with your own creative marketing plan, be patient, and GROW YOUR BUSINESS.

$ Money Saving Tip $
Need a free firewall, anti-virus, and anti-spyware software for your new business? Choose from many at **www.filehippo.com**. No technical support, but you can't beat the price.

Necessary Links

Customs website:
www.cbp.gov

19 CFR (Customs Regulations):
www.access.gpo.gov/cgi-bin/cfrassemble.cgi?title=201019
Note: replace "2010" with current year

Harmonized Tariff Schedule (HTS):
www.usitc.gov/tata/hts/bychapter/index.htm

Customs Forms:
www.cbp.gov/xp/cgov/toolbox/forms/

IRS Small Business:
www.irs.gov/businesses/small/index.html

$ Money Saving Tip $
Use the online format instead of a paper format CFR and HTS. The online editions are always up-to-date, will help to keep your office space clutter-free, and will save you money.

Start with Customs
Start Here

Customs Broker License

First, let's assume that you do have your customs broker license. If you don't, then let's get that first. Read part one of this book on how to become a customs broker. If you're already studying for the exam, then keep it up and good luck—the international shipping industry needs more licensed brokers and you're nearly there.

To Operate Under a Trade Name

Some individual customs brokers operate under their own personal names (e.g. John Doe). Others choose to give their small business a name (e.g. John Doe, DBA Perfect Customs Brokerage). Either way will work, but if you choose to operate under an assumed business name or DBA trade name, then Customs requires that the individual customs broker first submit a **proposal to operate under a trade name** in the form of a letter (**see sample on pg 77**, and see 19 CFR 111.30 (c) to verify information is up-to-date) to the Customs Broker Compliance Branch before proceeding with district permit application, filer code application, etc.

In your letter to Broker Compliance, refer to and attach evidence of your authority to use the trade name (usually in the form of your State's department of licensing confirmation letter or license). Also be sure to include your customs broker license number with this and all other such correspondence to Customs.

Customs will review your letter and will send back written approval to you within a couple weeks. They may be kind enough to email or fax confirmation back to you if politely asked to do so in your letter.

$ Money Saving Tip $
Computer a little outdated? Need to prolong its life? Take your computer to a "geek" or local computer store. They can upgrade your memory and suggest an external drive for more storage at a fraction of the price of a new computer.

Sample: ***Proposal to operate under a trade name***

John Doe
Perfect Customs Brokerage
3000 NE 309th Ave
Port City, WA 98682
Tel: 360-123-4567
johndoe@coldmail.com

(Date)

U.S. Customs and Border Protection
1300 Pennsylvania Ave., NW
Attn: 1400 L St., Broker Compliance Branch
Washington, DC 20229

Re: Proposal to operate under a trade name

Dear Sir or Madam,

Per 19 CFR 111.30 (c) I am submitting evidence of my authority to use the trade name (John Doe, DBA) **"Perfect Customs Brokerage"** per attached acknowledgement letter from the Washington State Department of Licensing (unified business identifier number 600000000).

Best Regards,

John Doe
License#12345

District Permit Request

A customs broker can only conduct customs business in the ports that he or she has permits for. The first permit that you will want to apply for is for the district in which you will initially be making customs entries.

A national permit can be applied for subsequent to receipt of the district permit. An individual customs broker may utilize remote location filing (RLF) if he or she has a national permit. RLF will allow you to make entry on regular informal or formal entry at any port even if you don't have an office at that port. Anyways, RLF is something to keep in mind and consider down the road. Just go to **www.cbp.gov** and search "remote location filing" for more information on the subject if you would like.

Include the following information in your **district permit application (see sample on pg 81)**...

§ Money Saving Tip §
Need another phone number with a different area code to extend your market into other localities? Pick up a prepaid cell phone just for that purpose.

1) Broker license number, date of issuance, and delivered through port (attach copy of license)

2) Your office address (attach copy of lease agreement or title)

3) Evidence of right to use assumed business name if applicable (attach approval from state)

4) Name of individual broker to exercise responsible supervision and control (usually your name)

5) List of other districts for which you have a permit (write "none" if none)

6) "Records retained at" address, and recordkeeping contact name

7) All other persons employed by applicant (write "none" if none)

8) Note $100.00 permit fee (attach check, and see 19 CFR 111.96 to verify amount is up-to-date).

9) Note $139.00 annual user fee (attach check, and see 19 CFR 111.96 to verify amount is up-to-date).

Be sure to make your checks out to "Customs and Border Protection". As of 2007, the 19 CFR still incorrectly instructs payments to be made out to the "United States Customs Service". Also be sure to time stamp and keep a copy of all such correspondence with Customs for your records.

$ Money Saving Tip $
Save money by slightly reducing the resolution on your printer. Go printer>>properties>> advanced. This prolongs the life of your ink or toner and you'll barely know the difference.

Sample: **District Permit Request**

John Doe
DBA Perfect Customs Brokerage
3000 NE 309th Ave
Port City, WA 98682
Tel: 360-123-4567
johndoe@coldmail.com

(Date)

Ms. Jane Smith, Port Director, CBP

Re: Application for District Permit for Port of Port City

Dear Ms. Smith,

Please accept this letter as application for a district permit to perform customs business in the port of Port City. Required information per CFR19, 111.19 (b) is as follows:

1) Broker License Number 12345, Date of issuance 4/22/05 (delivered through port of New Orleans, copy of license attached)
2) Office address: 3000 NE 309th Ave, Port City, WA 98682   Tel: 360-123-4567 (copy of lease attached)
3) Copy of document which reserves applicant's business name with the state of Washington (attached)
4) Individual broker to exercise responsible supervision and control: John Doe
5) Other districts for which I have a permit: None
6) Records retained at: 3000 NE 309th Ave, Port City, WA 98682. Recordkeeping contact: John Doe
7) All other persons employed by applicant: None
8) $100.00 permit fee (attached)
9) $138.00 annual user fee (attached)
Best Regards,

John Doe, **License#12345**

Filer Code Request

Each broker conducting business with Customs will be issued a three-letter code that will be notated with entry numbers for all customs entries. This three-letter code is called the filer code. To obtain a filer code, submit in a **filer code request** letter (separate from the district permit request), and include the following (**see sample on pg 84**)...

1) Full legal name of requestor (you)
2) Business contact (probably you)
3) Business address and telephone number
4) Broker license number, date of issuance, and "delivered through" port.

$ Money Saving Tip $
Need inexpensive accounting software to start off with? Try for free Microsoft Office Accounting Express or QuickBooks Simple Start Free Edition, and do a version upgrade when necessary at a later date.

The requests for district permit and filer code can be submitted together (verify with port director or equivalent just in case). They will provide you with a receipt for your checks, and will notify you of approval within about two to three weeks.

$ Money Saving Tip $

Some phonebook companies charge a substantial monthly fee to list in their yellow pages. However, there are many free print directories, and even more free online directories. They should provide all the phonebook exposure your company will need.

Sample: Filer Code Request

John Doe
DBA PERFECT Customs Brokerage
3000 NE 309th Ave
Port City, WA 98682
Tel: 360-123-4567
johndoe@coldmail.com

(Date)

Ms. Jane Smith
Port Director
Customs and Border Protection (Port of Port City)

Re: Filer Code Request

Dear Ms. Smith,

Please accept this letter as application for a filer code. Information required to process this application is as follows:

1) Full legal name of requestor: John Doe
2) Business contact (Individual broker to exercise responsible supervision and control): John Doe
3) Business address: 3000 NE 309th Ave, Port City, WA 98682 Tel: 360-123-4567
4) Broker License Number 12345, Date of issuance 4/22/05 (delivered through port of New Orleans)

Thank you very much for your consideration. Please feel free to contact me should you require further information.

Best Regards,

John Doe
License#12345

Type of Organization
Keep it simple

Legal Designation

While you're waiting for Customs to get back to you on your district permit and filer code applications, it may be a good time to focus on the structure of the business. Many large freight forwarder and customs brokerage operations are incorporated. For your start-up business, however, it may be best to keep it simple. By that I mean that I recommend registering your new business with your state as a sole proprietorship rather than an LLC or corporation.

I would not suggest a partnership for any type of business. I heard someone once say that "the partnership is the one ship that won't sail"? It's too difficult to make something work that equally involves the interests of more than one party, and hours worked and perceptions of contributions to the partnership will vary and eventually cause discontent and resentment.

As your business grows you can later decide to expand on your sole proprietorship by easily converting to an S-corporation. You can also purchase liability and/or errors and omissions insurance from an insurance or surety bond company to help protect your company.

Taxes

Taxes on your business will depend on several different factors, including legal designation, estimated income, and local tax code. It will be worth your money (about $100.00 a vist) and will give you peace of mind to consult with a recommended CPA in your area to understand your specific tax considerations.

One thing that every business owner must do, however, is to separate personal finances from business finances. This means setting up a separate bank account for your business. All business-related expenses come out of your business' account, and all business-related income goes into this account—no exceptions. Doing so will allow you to accurately compute your taxes, as well as let you know if your business is making a profit.

As a general rule of thumb, set aside about 1/3 of all withdrawn profits into yet another separate bank account (savings) for your business so that you have these funds available for taxes. So, if taking out $1,000.00 from your business' checking account, only $700.00 will go into your personal bank account, and the other $300.00 will go into and remain your business' savings account in preparation for tax time. Again, consult with a good CPA for details unique to your own situation.

An EIN (employee identification number) is not absolutely necessary to run your sole-proprietor business (as opposed of other forms of business), but some of your vendors may require it when applying for credit with them. You can get an EIN from the IRS if you wish by applying online at the following...

www.irs.gov/smallbiz/

The IRS's small business website also provides very informative online tutorials, among other useful tools. You can even sign up for a free newsletter to help keep you up-to-date on IRS happenings.

$ Money Saving Tip $
Use the EFTPS method of paying your IRS taxes. It is the quickest, most accurate, and the cheapest of method all. Go to **www.irs.gov/smallbiz** to learn more.

Marketing Your CHB Business
Get Creative

Still waiting for your district permit and filer code? Now is a perfect time to start working on your marketing plan.

You do not have to spend a lot of money to advertise your business. Here are just a few of the best methods of getting your business' name out there. And guess what? They're all FREE.

Customs Website

Ask your port director (or equivalent) if they can list your new business on CBP's list of brokers as soon as your filer code is created. All active brokers are listed by port on the Customs website (**www.cbp.gov**), and importers often search here first when looking for someone to clear their shipment. This may take a little patience and persistence, but the amount of exposure your company gets from this is well worth the wait.

Port Website

Most ports have a great website, which includes a directory of local warehouses, trucking companies, freight forwarders, and customs brokers. Contact your port (air, ocean, or both) and ask to be added to the list. This service should also be free, and is another great way to get a reference from a credible source.

Your Own Website

A legitimate online presence is essential. Luckily, Microsoft is generous enough to offer small business owners the opportunity to have their own advertisement-free domain name for FREE. There offering is called Microsoft Office Live, and I use it myself.

http://office.microsoft.com/en-US/officelive/default.aspx

You will first choose a domain name for your homepage and email address. Try to choose a fairly intuitive name that easily describes your service like PortTownCustomsBrokers.com, etc. Take your time in choosing your domain name. The reason being is that a creative domain name will help future customers more easily locate your website and remember your email address—two very vital parts of your marketing plan.

$ Money Saving Tip $
Making multiple trips to Customs? Deduct about 50¢ per mile as an expense. See **www.irs.gov/smallbiz** for the current rate.

Microsoft Office Live provides multiple useful functions such as an online submittal form on which customers can leave comments or inquiries that will be delivered directly to your email inbox, multiple email addresses, and a nifty website reporting tool that shows how much traffic your website is getting. Once it is up and running, register your website with Google and other popular search engines so that people can look for your business on the web.

Word of Mouth

A referral from a customer who has actually benefited from your quality product or service is a nice compliment. It is also one of the most convincing forms of advertisement for your business. Don't hesitate to ask your clients to refer your customs brokerage business to their friends and colleagues. Customer testimonials on your website can also help to win the trust of a prospective client.

Other Marketing Advice

I also recommend the book *Guerilla Marketing* by Jay Conrad Levinson. This book is chalk-full of winning ideas to advertise your on-a-budget business. It is extensive in its description of all different kinds of marketing techniques. The book will pay for itself.

ABI Vendor
Test Drive it for the Right Fit

Selecting an ABI Vendor

Choosing an ABI provider is easy. Choosing the best ABI provider for your company takes some shopping around.

An initial one-time licensing fee will run anywhere from $10,000.00 to $2,000.00. After that, monthly maintenance fees for ABI providers can be as expensive as $1,000.00 per month or as low as $200.00 per month. Most offer a full array of ABI capabilities, but of course some offer more accounting and other optional features than others. Some require you to buy a server to run off of, while others allow you to do everything online thru the use of their server—as if you were creating and sending an email in your Hotmail or Yahoo! Mail email account.

$ Money Saving Tip $
Want the most out of your printer? Consider picking up a multi-function device that will allow you to print, copy, scan, and fax in a compact package.

My best advice to you is to shop around for the best price, and make sure you compare the actual functionality of two or three different vendors with actual one-on-one demo's (either in-person or online). Also, get a good feel for a company's culture. Your instincts may tell you whether they will offer superior or below-average customer service when (not if) you have a question or problem with their system.

A current listing of all ABI vendors, certified by US Customs, can by searching for "abi software vendors list" on **www.cbp.gov**.

$ Money Saving Tip $
Thinking of printing your own business cards or promotional material? Outsource this to a local printing company? This is the most cost effective way.

Reproducing Customs Forms

The Customs Forms Management Office in Washington, DC requires all ABI providers to submit their versions of US Customs forms (3461, 7501, etc.) to their office for approval before the forms are printed by individual brokers (via their laser or inkjet printers). Customs is concerned that their forms be kept uniform, and Customs may request this letter of approval at anytime.

Interestingly enough, not all ABI providers seem have this important letter of proof, so it is important to request (not ask) that your ABI provider of choice to provide a copy of this letter for your file before you commit to buying their product.

$ Money Saving Tip $
The ABI provider will charge for a one-time license fee and a monthly maintenance fee. Ask for some wiggle room on the monthly maintenance fee, and most will be willing to negotiate with you on this.

Letter of Intent

Once you have received your district permit and filer code from Customs, you will ask the ABI provider to provide a letter of intent template (**see sample on pg 95,** and see 19 CFR 143 to verify information is up-to-date) that you or your ABI provider can send to the Customs Office of Information and Technology (OIT). The only thing that you will need to add to the template should be your new filer code and a signature. Have the letter of intent mailed to the OIT or call them at (703) 650-3500 to ask if you can fax the letter in order to expedite the process. Make sure that your ABI provider also gets a copy of the submitted letter. Go to **www.cbp.gov** and type "getting started with ABI" for current instructions in detail.

§ Money Saving Tip §
Want to gain a little interest on your business' checking account? Go to **checkingfinder.com** to find banks with the best rates and other attractive extras. Rates reaching nearly 5%.

Sample: ABI Letter of Intent

John Doe
Perfect Customs Brokerage
3000 NE 309th Ave
Port City, WA 98682
Tel: 360-123-4567
johndoe@coldmail.com

(Date)

Office of Information and Technology
Director of Client Representatives Branch
7501 Boston Blvd. 2nd Floor, Room 211
Springfield, VA 22153

RE: Letter of intent to participation in ACS/ABI.

Per 19 CFR 143.2, this letter of intent sets forth our commitment to develop, maintain and adhere to the performance requirements and operational standards of the ABI system in order to ensure the validity, integrity and confidentiality of the data transmitted.

1)   The following is a description of the computer hardware, communications and entry processing systems to be used and the estimated completion date of the programming: (**ABI provider will advise these details**).
2)   Our offices are located at: 3000 NE 309th Ave Port City, WA 98682. Contact: John Doe.
3)   The name of the participant's principal management and contact person regarding the system: John Doe
4)   The system is being developed by the following data processing company: PDQ Systems. Contact: Denise Richards
5)   Entry filer code: XYZ

Please feel free to contact us should you have any questions.

Best regards,

John Doe, LCB, License#12345

The letter of intent will be processed in about a week. Customs will assign an ABI representative to you. He or she will contact you to introduce themselves, and you can advise your ISA confirmation number (**see next**) at that time as well. Once an ABI rep is assigned, you will work closely with him or her and your ABI provider to test your ABI transmissions. Ask your ABI provider to help you prepare for and walk you through this ABI testing period, which can be completed within a couple days (depending on your provider).

VPN Interconnection Security Agreement

The Trade Virtual Private Network (VPN) Interconnection Security Agreement (ISA) is how Customs informs the ABI applicant of the importance of keeping the connection between your computer and Customs secure. Go to the following online form, read the agreement, and complete and submit the security agreement acceptance form.

https://apps.cbp.gov/tvpn/tvpn.asp

Once submitted you will receive a confirmation number via email. Simply reply to the confirmation email from Customs to complete the ISA acceptance process. Keep this confirmation number and advise it to your ABI representative when they contact you.

Selecting a Surety Company
That was Easy

The surety company that you choose will be able to issue single transaction bonds and continuous bonds to accompany your customs entries.

Before deciding on a surety company, check with your ABI provider to see if they integrate a specific company's bonds in their system. If they do, and if the surety's rates are reasonable, then use them.

Otherwise, selecting a surety company can still be much easier than selecting an ABI provider as prices seem to be relatively similar between competing companies. Ask for a few quotes to get a better idea of what's out there.

$ Money Saving Tip $
Want shipping industry news for free? Sign up for the Journal of Commerce's free newsletter at **www.joc.com**

I would recommend choosing a surety company that does not charge a minimum for your single transaction bonds, and one that has an easy-to-use bond application system. Some may let you get your single transaction bonds directly online, while others will have you download software that will allow you to issue bonds directly from your desktop.

Search for "surety names/codes" on **www.cbp.gov** to get a current listing of Customs approved surety companies that can provide you a quote.

Running Your CHB Business
Do it Differently

The day-to-day operations of your new customs brokerage business is entirely up to you. You can get as creative as you want. That's to your advantage, because most of the customs brokerage businesses out there are doing the same thing.

Power of Attorney

A signed power of attorney (POA) from the importer is required in order for a customs broker to conduct customs business on behalf of that importer.

As an individual customs broker, you can do one of two things (that I am aware of). You can choose to purchase a standard or specialized power of attorney from a forms provider. The National Customs Brokers & Freight Forwarders Association of America (NCBFFAA), for example has published several different versions of the power of attorney for the transportation industry. They can be purchased at Apperson Print Management Services located on the web at **http://www.appersonprint.com/**.

Your other option is to take a look at Customs' example of the power of attorney as written in 19 CFR 141.31, and customize it to fit your company (**see sample on pg 101**). I recommend this method as it is FREE, faster, and less intimidating to customers than the long form provided by the NCBFFAA.

And as you have your customer fill out the power of attorney, ask them to also complete and return what I call the "customers instructions to broker" (**see sample on pg 102**). The importer can use this form to describe their imported product, and clarify delivery and billing details. This lets your new client know that you care about their input, and provides the additional information that you will need to take care of their shipment.

$ Money Saving Tip $
Looking for extremely cheap office furniture and equipment? Visit **Craigslist.org** or your local paper's classifieds bargain section. You won't believe all the stuff you can get for free.

Customs Power of Attorney

KNOW ALL MEN BY THESE PRESENTS, THAT

_____

(Full name of company or individual)

_____

(Legal designation, such as corp., individual, sole prop., LLC, or partnership)
located at

_____

(Business Address)
and doing business under the laws of the State of

_____, using EIN or SSN_____
hereby appoints the grantee, **John Doe, DBA Perfect Customs Brokerage** as a true and lawful agent and attorney of the principal named above with full power and authority to do and perform every lawful act and thing the said agent and attorney may deem requisite and necessary to be done for and on behalf of the said principal without limitation of any kind as fully as said principal could do if present and acting, and hereby ratify and confirm all that said agent and attorney shall lawfully do or cause to be done by virtue of these presents until written notice of revocation is delivered to the grantee. In the case of a partnership, this power of attorney will only be effective two years from the date below.

_____   _____

(Principal's signature)   *(Date)*

Customer Instructions to Broker

1) The product that I am importing can best be described as...

_____
(What is it? What is it made of?)

_____
(What is it used for? What is it used in conjunction with?)

2) Please deliver to...

_____
(delivery address)

_____
(delivery location contact name and telephone#)

This location **does / doesn't** have a loading dock. *(Pls circle one)*

3) Please bill to...

_____
(billing address)

_____
(billing contact name and telephone#)

ACH Payment

Complete Customs Form 401 (ACH Credit Enrollment Application) and fax, email, or mail the completed application to the Customs Revenue Division. Upon receipt, they will send instructions to you on ACH payer procedures as well as show you how to send an ACH pre-note test (necessary for ACH user approval) through your bank to Customs. Go to **www.cbp.gov** and type "signing up for ach" for details and current instructions. Once approved, you can work with your ABI provider and bank to set everything else up. Until then, Customs will accept checks submitted with the entry or entry summary.

Accounting Software

If you're not a seasoned CPA (like the rest of us), then keeping track of your company's finances requires accounting software that is easy to use. If your ABI provider offers accounting software with their product, then feel free to use it as that may help simplify things.

If they do not offer integrated software, then stand-along accounting software such as QuickBooks will work as well. Because of its widespread use, many ABI providers include functions in the ABI software that allow you to easily transfer data to and from QuickBooks.

Pricing

Be aware of your competitors' pricing. You may want to beat their pricing and/or offer importers a much more simplified version of the typical customs brokerage invoice. If you can boast about your great rates then feel free to compare yours to the "typical" customs broker on your website or via other methods of advertising.

Creativity can also enter into your method of pricing of your customs brokerage services. You might not have the cash on hand that a larger business has, so you could offer a substantial discount to an importer if he or she submits payment to you at the time of or before delivery of her shipment. This will help you to cash flow your business, and give you a chance to go out and meet your customers.

Truckers

Contact several different truckers and get an account setup with them before your first shipment. Most will require you to complete a credit check application, while others will ask for payment to be made on a COD basis for the first couple of shipments. Either way, it is nice to have a trusting friend in your trucking company.

Necessary Office Equipment

You only really need a computer, printer, telephone, and shredder (Customs requires all information-sensitive material to be shredded rather than put in the dumpster) to start operating your new business.

To improve on your productivity, you may want to invest in an inexpensive ($200.00 or so) all-in-one (laser printer, scanner, copier, fax). A broadband connection may also be necessary, but check with your ABI provider to make sure. The point is that you don't need a lot of money to start things up—just be patient in your accumulation of office equipment and supplies.

$ Money Saving Tip $
Cleared a small shipment and free on time? Deliver using your own car or rent a truck (your car insurance co. may have weight restrictions). This is a good chance to see your customer and really boosts your profits.

Some other items that you might want to consider as your business grows may include...

- Separate external hard drive for data backup

- Cordless phone with speakerphone and a jack for a headset

- Rolodex for old-fashioned contact organization

- Extra phone line for business use

Recordkeeping

Customs requires brokers to keep records (either in paper or electronic form) of transaction for five years. The IRS requires an individual or business to keep tax-related records for three years (I recommend keeping longer).

! Final Tip !
Finally, I recommend that you don't use debt to finance your business. Grow the business with a patient heart.

However, there is no need to invest in a row of file cabinets if you're on a budget. Just go to Wal-Mart and buy folder files, some hanging files to organize them in, and a few banker boxes to hang the hanging files in. Not only is this method cheaper, but the banker boxes are easier to move around and store.

Wal-Mart, by the way, is usually the most affordable place to buy your office supplies (paper, pens, etc.).

Working with Customs

Customs doesn't care whether the customs broker that is submitting an entry to them works for the largest carrier in America, or whether he or she is working off a ten dollar coffee table in the corner of their apartment. Just do your best to build a reputation as an honest and straight-forward broker, and Customs will treat you fairly.

Also, it goes without saying, but be aware that Customs is a government institution and things take time (including their role in processing your before-mentioned applications).

Finally, I would like to wish you the best of luck on your customs broker exam if you are preparing to take it and on your customs brokerage business and career.

References

Office of the Federal Register. National Archives and Records Administration. "Customs Duties" Title 19 Code of Federal Regulations, Chapter I. Washington: Government Printing Office, April 1, 2009 ed., www.access.gpo.gov. Web. 21 February 2010.

U.S. Department of Homeland Security. Customs and Border Protection. "Exam and Key Downloads" www.cbp.gov. Web. 21 February 2010.

Index

Made in the USA
Lexington, KY
22 September 2011